WELCOME TO THE U.S.A.

TENNESSEE

Written by Ann Heinrichs   Illustrated by Matt Kania
Content Adviser: Carroll Van West, Director, Center for Historic
Preservation at Middle Tennessee State University and Director,
Tennessee Civil War National Heritage Area,
Murfreesboro, Tennessee

The Child's World

Published in the United States of America by The Child's World®
PO Box 326 • Chanhassen, MN 55317-0326
800-599-READ • www.childsworld.com

Photo Credits
Cover: Tennessee Department of Tourism Development; frontispiece: Getty Images/Photodisc/Kim Steele.

Interior: American Museum of Science and Energy: 22; AP/Wide World Photo/Mark Humphrey: 10; Bell Buckle Chamber of Commerce: 34; Corbis: 9 (Raymond Gehman), 25 (John Madere), 26 (Chase Swift); Mayfield Dairy: 33; Rocky Mount Museum: 14; State of Tennessee: 13; Tennessee Department of Tourism Development: 6, 17, 21, 29, 30; Tennessee Valley Authority: 18.

Acknowledgments
The Child's World®: Mary Berendes, Publishing Director

Editorial Directions, Inc.: E. Russell Primm, Editorial Director; Katie Marsico, Associate Editor; Judith Shiffer, Assistant Editor; Matt Messbarger, Editorial Assistant; Susan Hindman, Copy Editor; Melissa McDaniel, Proofreader; Kevin Cunningham, Peter Garnham, Matt Messbarger, Olivia Nellums, Chris Simms, Molly Symmonds, Katherine Trickle, Carl Stephen Wender, Fact Checkers; Tim Griffin/IndexServ, Indexer; Cian Loughlin O'Day, Photo Researcher and Editor

The Design Lab: Kathleen Petelinsek, Design; Julia Goozen, Art Production

Library of Congress Cataloging-in-Publication Data
Heinrichs, Ann.
  Tennessee / by Ann Heinrichs ; cartography and illustrations by Matt Kania.
    p. cm. — (Welcome to the U.S.A.)
  Includes index.
  ISBN 1-59296-484-2 (library bound : alk. paper) 1. Tennessee—Juvenile literature.
I. Kania, Matt, ill. II. Title.
  F436.3.H45 2006
  976.8—dc22   2005012091

Ann Heinrichs is the author of more than 100 books for children and young adults. She has also enjoyed successful careers as a children's book editor and an advertising copywriter. Ann grew up in Fort Smith, Arkansas, and lives in Chicago, Illinois.

About the Author
Ann Heinrichs

Matt Kania loves maps and, as a kid, dreamed of making them. In school he studied geography and cartography, and today he makes maps for a living. Matt's favorite thing about drawing maps is learning about the places they represent. Many of the maps he has created can be found in books, magazines, videos, Web sites, and public places.

About the
Map Illustrator
Matt Kania

On the cover: Climb to the top of Lookout Mountain for a great view of Chattanooga!
On page one: Listen to some great music at the Country Jam in Nashville!

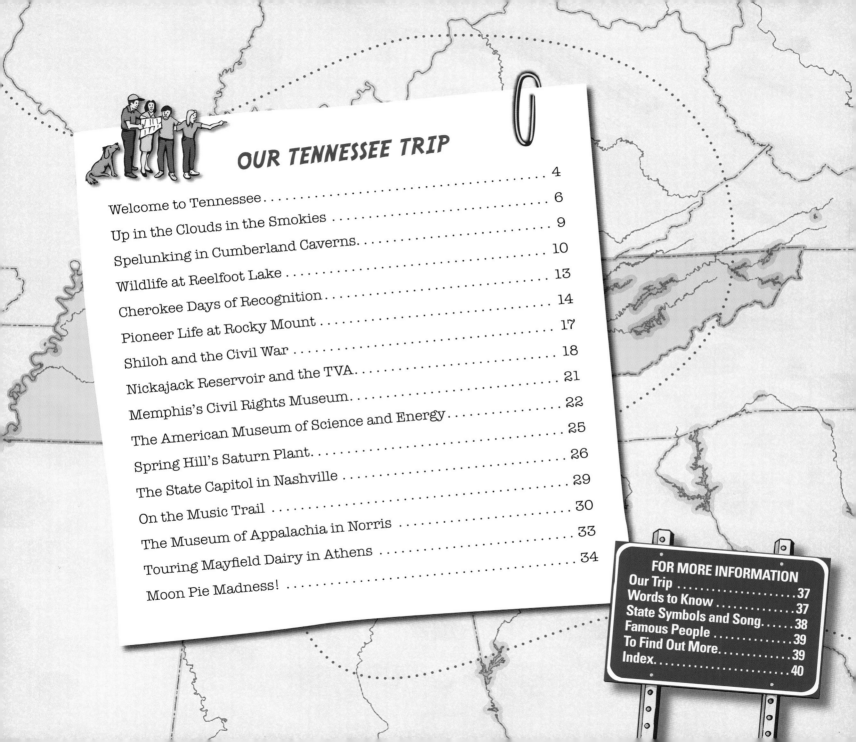

OUR TENNESSEE TRIP

Tennessee's Nickname:
The Volunteer State

Let's explore Tennessee! It's a great state for adventure and fun.

What will you do in Tennessee? You'll meet **robots,** turtles, and tree frogs. You'll hang out with soldiers in tent camps. You'll see how cars and ice cream are made. You'll hear mountain fiddlers and American Indian storytellers. You'll float lazily down a river. And you'll explore caves and eat Moon Pies!

We'd better get started, so buckle up. It's time to hit the road!

WELCOME TO TENNESSEE

As you travel through Tennessee, watch for all the interesting facts along the way.

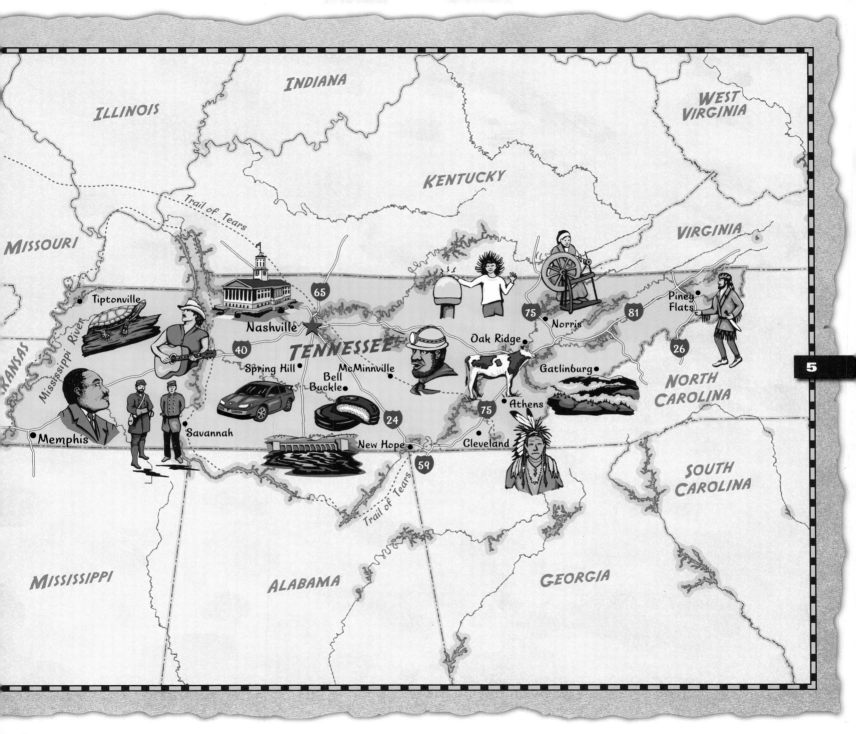

ILLINOIS

INDIANA

WEST VIRGINIA

MISSOURI

KENTUCKY

VIRGINIA

Trail of Tears

65

Piney Flats

Tiptonville

81

26

75

NORTH CAROLINA

Nashville

Norris

40

Oak Ridge

TENNESSEE

Spring Hill

Gatlinburg

ARKANSAS

Mississippi River

McMinnville

Bell Buckle

75

Athens

Savannah

24

Cleveland

Memphis

New Hope

59

SOUTH CAROLINA

Trail of Tears

5

MISSISSIPPI

ALABAMA

GEORGIA

The Smoky Mountains are great for hiking. Grab your walking stick and hit the trail!

Up in the Clouds in the Smokies

Wander through the Great Smoky Mountains. They're called the Smokies for short. You'll see why they have this name. Low-hanging clouds are all around you. They look like smoke!

The Smokies are part of the Blue Ridge Mountains. These mountains run down Tennessee's eastern edge.

West of here is the valley. The Tennessee River flows through it. Next is the rocky Cumberland Plateau.

The Highland Rim is like a big bowl. At the bottom is the Nashville Basin. Then comes another section of the Tennessee River. The Mississippi River forms Tennessee's western border.

The Mississippi River Museum is in Memphis's Mud Island River Park. It has a working model of the Mississippi River. It shows the river's course to the Gulf of Mexico.

Cumberland Gap National Historical Park is near Harrogate. Tennessee, Virginia, and Kentucky meet at this point. **Pioneers** once crossed the mountains through the gap.

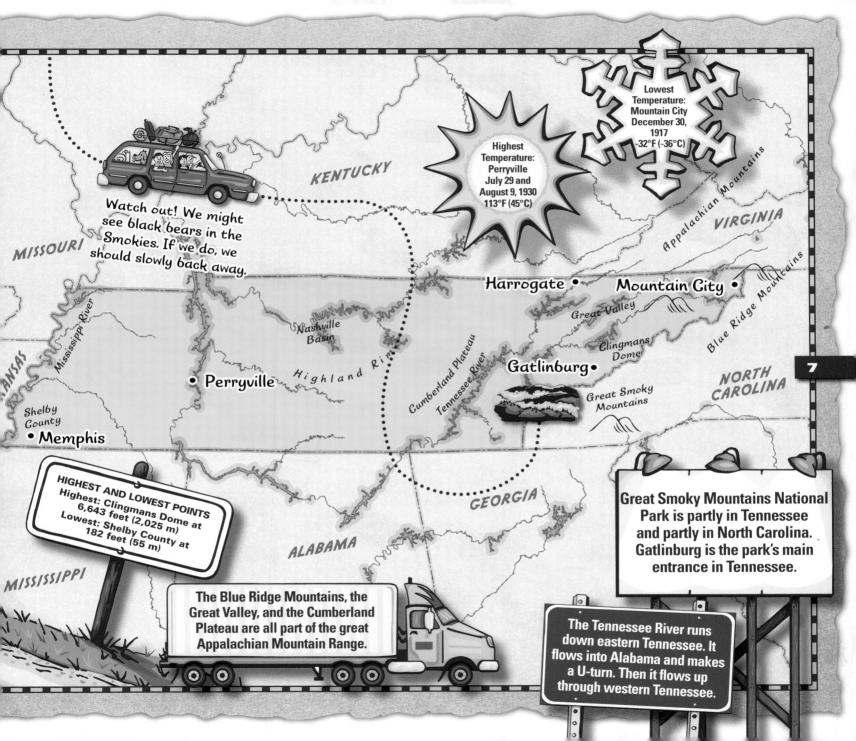

Watch out! We might see black bears in the Smokies. If we do, we should slowly back away.

Lowest Temperature: Mountain City December 30, 1917 -32°F (-36°C)

Highest Temperature: Perryville July 29 and August 9, 1930 113°F (45°C)

KENTUCKY

VIRGINIA

Appalachian Mountains

MISSOURI

Harrogate •

Mountain City •

Great Valley

Blue Ridge Mountains

Nashville Basin

Clingmans Dome

Cumberland Plateau

NORTH CAROLINA

• Perryville

Highland Rim

Tennessee River

Gatlinburg •

Mississippi River

Great Smoky Mountains

Shelby County

• Memphis

HIGHEST AND LOWEST POINTS
Highest: Clingmans Dome at 6,643 feet (2,025 m)
Lowest: Shelby County at 182 feet (55 m)

GEORGIA

Great Smoky Mountains National Park is partly in Tennessee and partly in North Carolina. Gatlinburg is the park's main entrance in Tennessee.

MISSISSIPPI

ALABAMA

The Blue Ridge Mountains, the Great Valley, and the Cumberland Plateau are all part of the great Appalachian Mountain Range.

The Tennessee River runs down eastern Tennessee. It flows into Alabama and makes a U-turn. Then it flows up through western Tennessee.

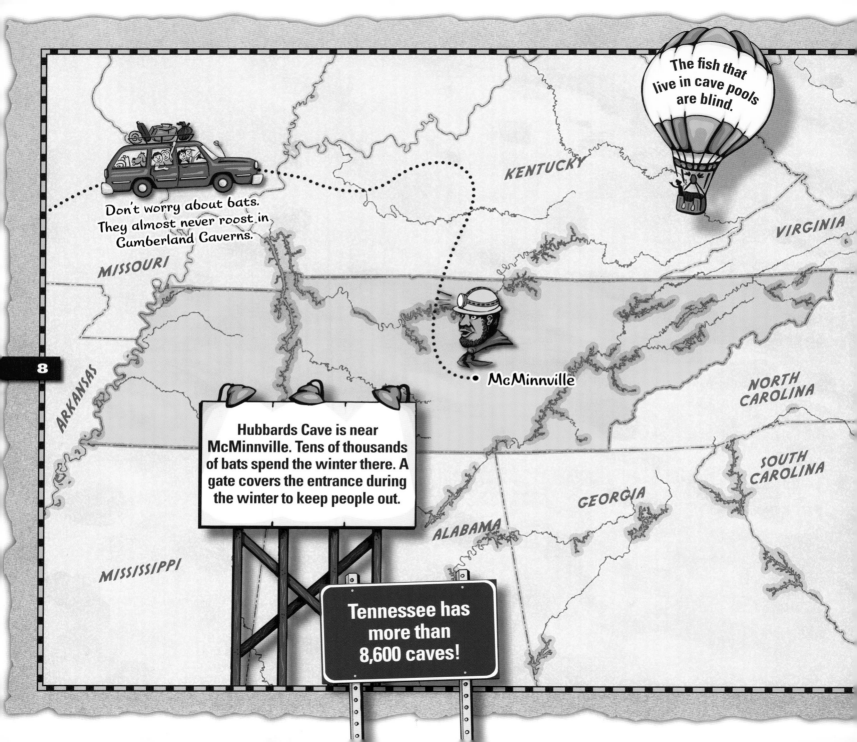

The fish that live in cave pools are blind.

Don't worry about bats. They almost never roost in Cumberland Caverns.

KENTUCKY

VIRGINIA

MISSOURI

McMinnville

NORTH CAROLINA

ARKANSAS

Hubbards Cave is near McMinnville. Tens of thousands of bats spend the winter there. A gate covers the entrance during the winter to keep people out.

SOUTH CAROLINA

GEORGIA

ALABAMA

MISSISSIPPI

Tennessee has more than 8,600 caves!

Spelunking in Cumberland Caverns

Want to go spelunking? That means exploring caves! Check out Cumberland **Caverns,** near McMinnville. It's Tennessee's longest cave system. Its underground rooms are awesome! One is called the Hall of the Mountain King. It's as long as two football fields!

Wander along the winding passageways. You'll view underground waterfalls and pools. You'll see walls covered with moon milk. That's a bubbly looking white rock. And you'll spot gypsum flowers. These rock formations look like curly vines. When you're done, you'll be an expert spelunker!

The rock formations in Cumberland Caverns are really cool. Just be sure to bring a flashlight!

The Tennessee cave salamander is Tennessee's official state amphibian. Amphibians are able to live both on land and in water.

A stinkpot is a musk turtle. It can release a stinky substance to defend itself.

Keep your eyes to the skies! You may spot an eagle soaring high overhead!

Reelfoot Lake is Tennessee's largest natural lake. It was created when earthquakes struck in 1811 and 1812.

Wildlife at Reelfoot Lake

Want to see some sliders and stinkpots? They're types of turtles! How about river otters? They swim on their backs in the lake. Little green tree frogs are hopping around, too.

You're exploring Reelfoot National Wildlife Refuge! It surrounds Reelfoot Lake. That's in Tennessee's northwest corner, near Tiptonville.

Tennessee has many mountains, forests, rivers, and lakes. And they're full of wildlife! Deer and wild turkeys live there. You'll spot beavers, raccoons, rabbits, and skunks. You'll even see wild hogs in the mountains. Steer clear! They can have a nasty temper!

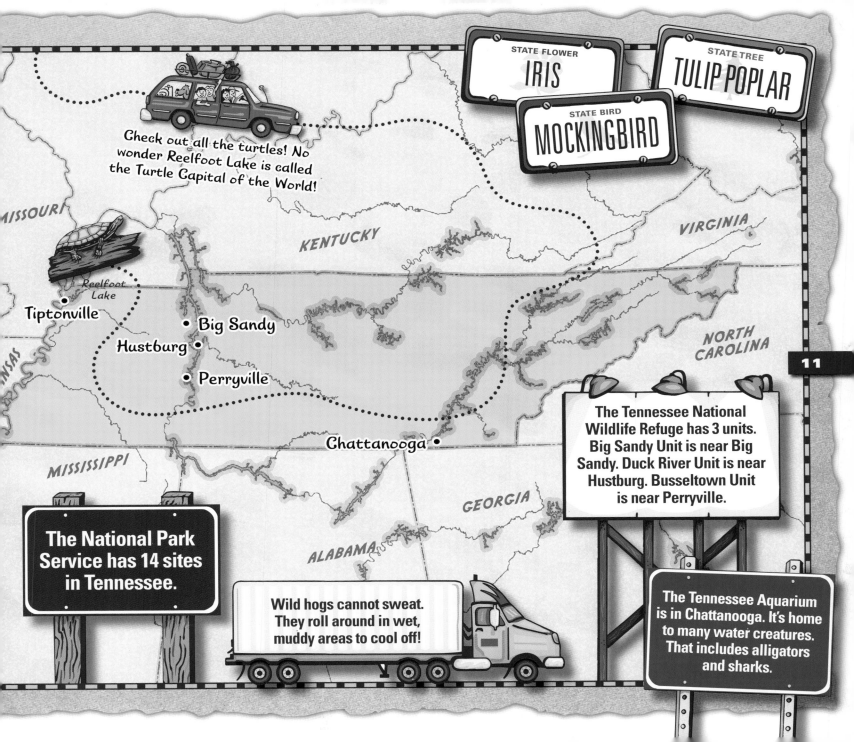

Check out all the turtles! No wonder Reelfoot Lake is called the Turtle Capital of the World!

MISSOURI

KENTUCKY

VIRGINIA

NORTH CAROLINA

Reelfoot Lake

Tiptonville

Big Sandy

Hustburg

Perryville

ARKANSAS

Chattanooga

MISSISSIPPI

GEORGIA

ALABAMA

The Tennessee National Wildlife Refuge has 3 units. Big Sandy Unit is near Big Sandy. Duck River Unit is near Hustburg. Busseltown Unit is near Perryville.

The National Park Service has 14 sites in Tennessee.

Wild hogs cannot sweat. They roll around in wet, muddy areas to cool off!

The Tennessee Aquarium is in Chattanooga. It's home to many water creatures. That includes alligators and sharks.

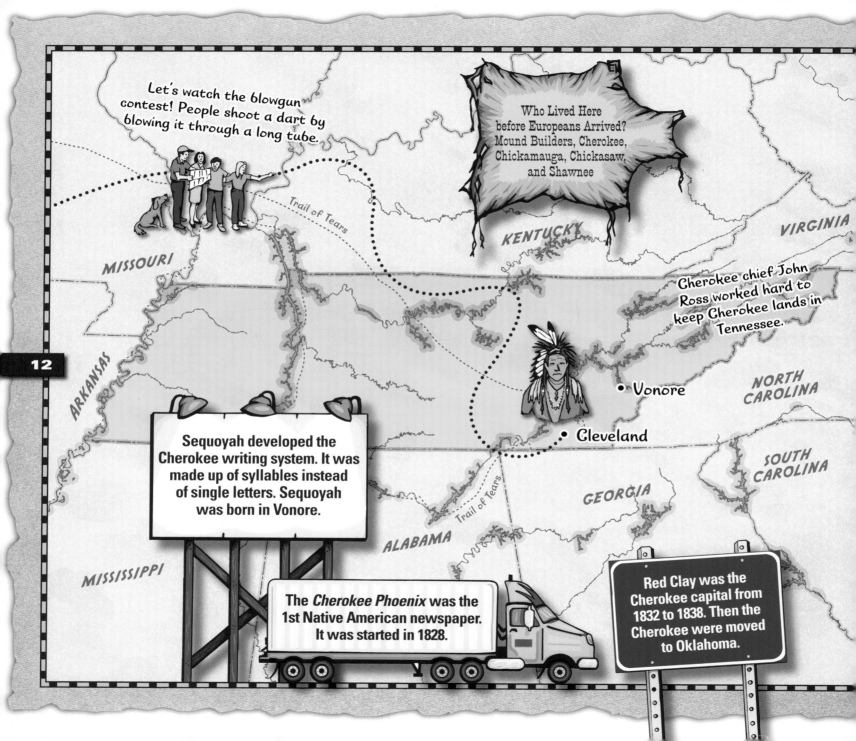

Cherokee Days of Recognition

Tap your feet to the steady drumbeat. Watch the fancy dancers leap and swirl. Hear storytellers tell their ancient tales.

You're attending the Cherokee Days of Recognition! It's in Red Clay State Park. That's right on the Georgia border south of Cleveland.

Red Clay was once the Cherokee capital. The Cherokee were very accomplished. They published a Cherokee-language newspaper. But the U.S. government wanted Cherokee lands. The Cherokee and other Indians were moved west. They were sent to Indian Territory in Oklahoma. Their sad journey is called the Trail of Tears.

Want to learn about Native American culture? Then check out the Cherokee Days of Recognition!

The name *Tennessee* comes from a Cherokee village called Tanasie.

Pioneer Life at Rocky Mount

Want to attend a pioneer wedding? Catch a reenactment at Rocky Mount Museum!

Davy Crockett was a famous woodsman. He was born near Limestone.

Step into the log cabin. It was built in 1791. Make your way to the kitchen. Try some gingerbread cooked over an open fire. Then visit the weaving cabin. You'll see how people spun and wove wool.

You're exploring Rocky Mount Museum. It's in Piney Flats. There you'll see how Tennessee pioneers lived.

Pioneers were really tough. They crossed the mountains into the wilderness. They chopped down trees to build homes.

Woodsman Daniel Boone cut a trail for pioneers. He began near Kingsport in 1775. Then he continued on to Virginia and Kentucky. This was called the Wilderness Trail.

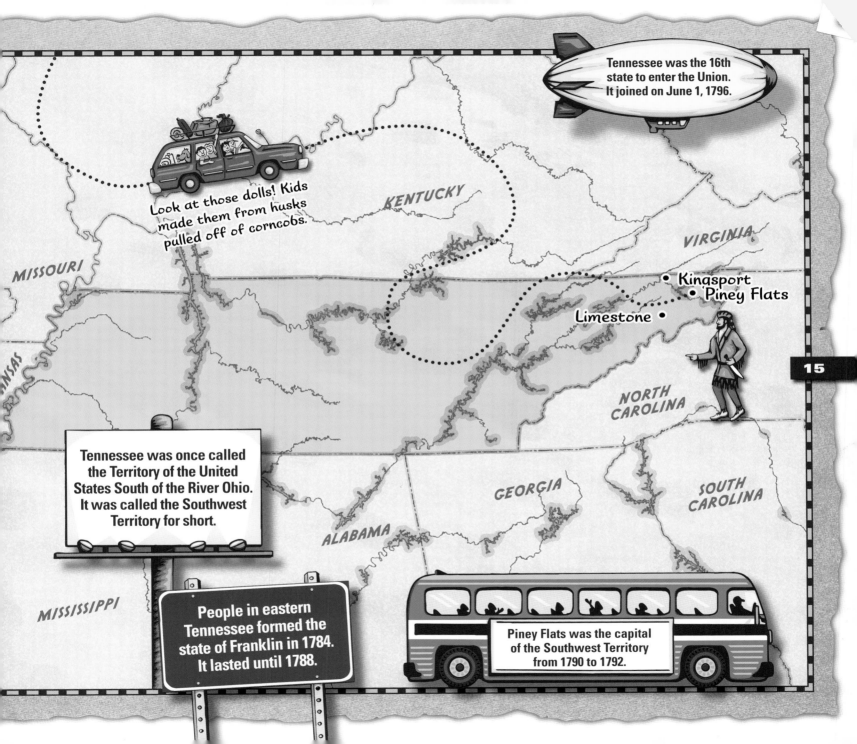

Tennessee was the 16th state to enter the Union. It joined on June 1, 1796.

Look at those dolls! Kids made them from husks pulled off of corncobs.

• Kingsport
• Piney Flats

Limestone •

Tennessee was once called the Territory of the United States South of the River Ohio. It was called the Southwest Territory for short.

People in eastern Tennessee formed the state of Franklin in 1784. It lasted until 1788.

Piney Flats was the capital of the Southwest Territory from 1790 to 1792.

KENTUCKY

VIRGINIA

MISSOURI

NORTH CAROLINA

GEORGIA

SOUTH CAROLINA

ALABAMA

MISSISSIPPI

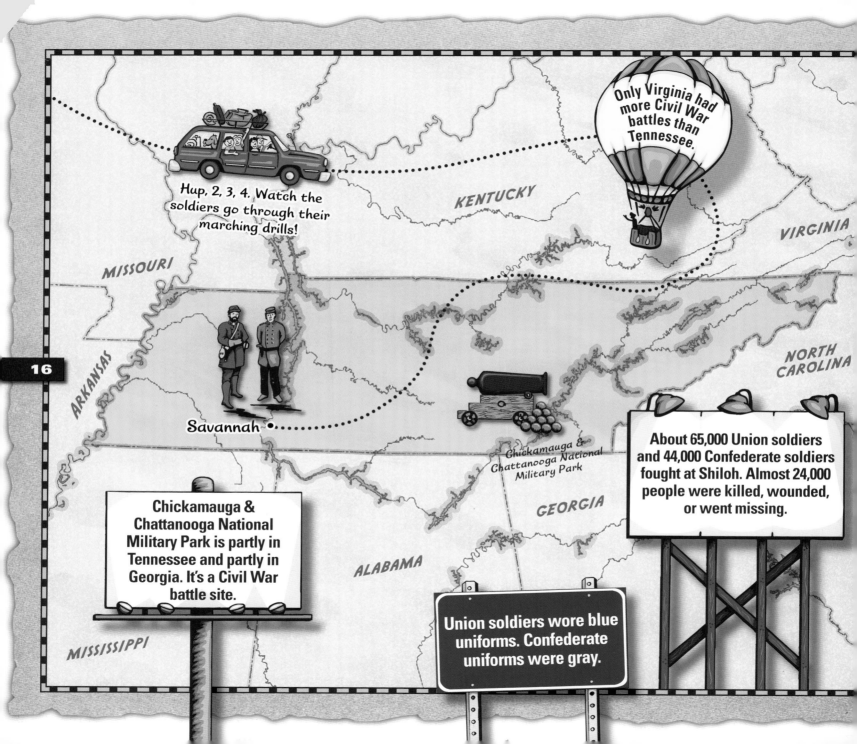

Only Virginia had more Civil War battles than Tennessee.

Hup, 2, 3, 4. Watch the soldiers go through their marching drills!

KENTUCKY

VIRGINIA

MISSOURI

ARKANSAS

NORTH CAROLINA

Savannah

Chickamauga & Chattanooga National Military Park

About 65,000 Union soldiers and 44,000 Confederate soldiers fought at Shiloh. Almost 24,000 people were killed, wounded, or went missing.

Chickamauga & Chattanooga National Military Park is partly in Tennessee and partly in Georgia. It's a Civil War battle site.

GEORGIA

ALABAMA

Union soldiers wore blue uniforms. Confederate uniforms were gray.

MISSISSIPPI

Shiloh and the Civil War

Visit with soldiers in their tent camps. Some wear blue uniforms, and some wear gray. They show how they fired their guns and cannons.

You're at Shiloh battlefield near Savannah. People are honoring the **anniversary** of this battle. It took place during the Civil War (1861–1865).

This war divided the nation. The North, or Union side, opposed slavery. The South, or Confederacy, wanted to keep slavery. There were Tennesseans on both sides. But Tennessee ended up joining the Confederacy. Many battles were fought in Tennessee. At last, the Union won. Tennessee was the first state to rejoin the Union.

Drummers honor the anniversary of the battle at Shiloh.

The Battle of Shiloh took place on April 6–7, 1862. The Union side won a big victory there.

Nickajack Reservoir and the TVA

Grab a paddle and head for the water. There's plenty to do at Nickajack Reservoir!

Tennessee has 14 lakes created by TVA dams. They're in the Tennessee River valley.

Want to learn to paddle a canoe? How about a lazy float on an inner tube? You can do all this at Nickajack **Reservoir.**

These waters weren't always so smooth. There were dangerous stretches with scary names. One was called the Boiling Pot! Boats could easily get wrecked there.

Nickajack Reservoir was created by damming a river. Tennessee has many other dams. The Tennessee Valley Authority (TVA) built most of them.

The TVA was established in 1933. TVA dams control floods and soil **erosion.** They make rough waters safe for boats. They also provide electric power over wide areas.

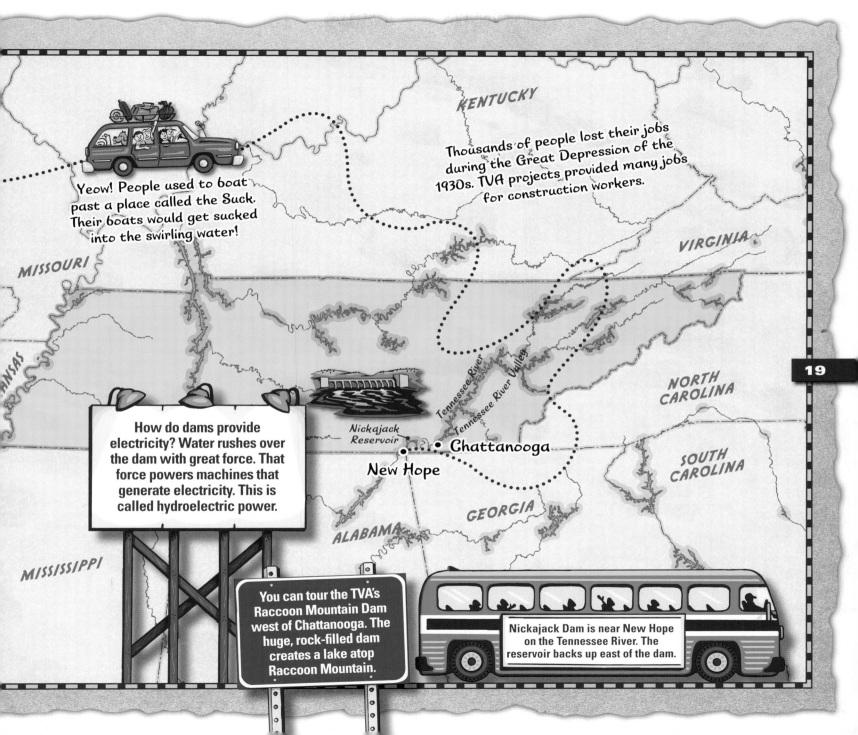

Yeow! People used to boat past a place called the Suck. Their boats would get sucked into the swirling water!

Thousands of people lost their jobs during the Great Depression of the 1930s. TVA projects provided many jobs for construction workers.

How do dams provide electricity? Water rushes over the dam with great force. That force powers machines that generate electricity. This is called hydroelectric power.

You can tour the TVA's Raccoon Mountain Dam west of Chattanooga. The huge, rock-filled dam creates a lake atop Raccoon Mountain.

Nickajack Dam is near New Hope on the Tennessee River. The reservoir backs up east of the dam.

Nickajack Reservoir

Chattanooga

New Hope

Tennessee River

Tennessee River Valley

KENTUCKY

VIRGINIA

MISSOURI

NORTH CAROLINA

SOUTH CAROLINA

GEORGIA

ALABAMA

MISSISSIPPI

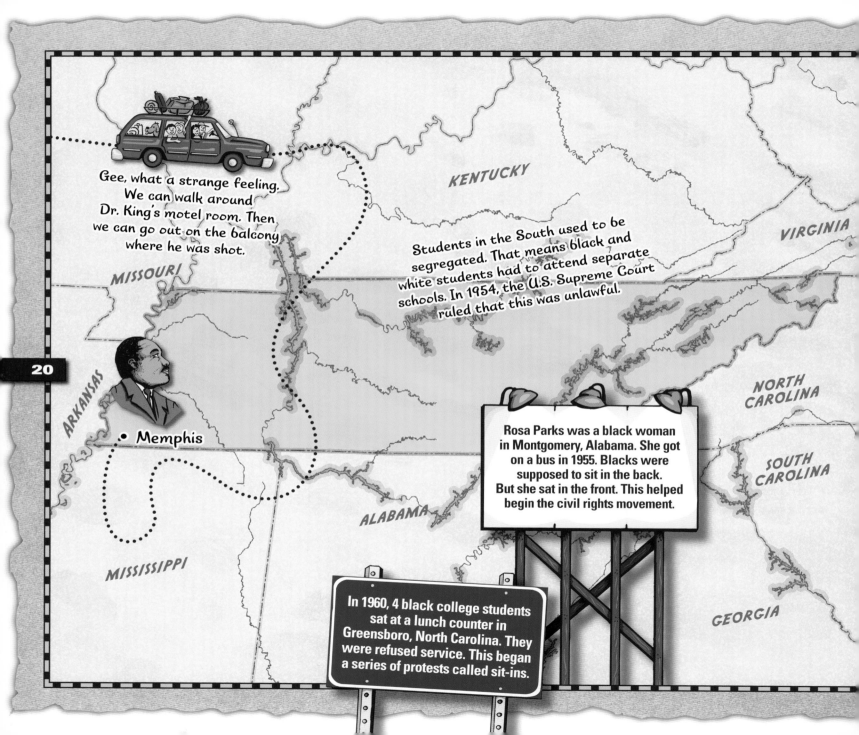

Gee, what a strange feeling. We can walk around Dr. King's motel room. Then we can go out on the balcony where he was shot.

KENTUCKY

VIRGINIA

Students in the South used to be segregated. That means black and white students had to attend separate schools. In 1954, the U.S. Supreme Court ruled that this was unlawful.

MISSOURI

ARKANSAS

• Memphis

NORTH CAROLINA

Rosa Parks was a black woman in Montgomery, Alabama. She got on a bus in 1955. Blacks were supposed to sit in the back. But she sat in the front. This helped begin the civil rights movement.

SOUTH CAROLINA

ALABAMA

MISSISSIPPI

GEORGIA

In 1960, 4 black college students sat at a lunch counter in Greensboro, North Carolina. They were refused service. This began a series of protests called sit-ins.

Memphis's Civil Rights Museum

Take your seat at the lunch counter. You'll see how blacks were treated there. They were protesting a "whites-only" rule. Then sit at the front of a bus. A voice orders you to move to the back. You're visiting the National **Civil Rights** Museum.

Many exhibits feature Dr. Martin Luther King Jr. Why? Because the museum building was once the Lorraine Motel. Dr. King was shot and killed there in 1968. The museum has a hopeful message, though. It shows that Dr. King's dreams live on.

He dreamed that all people could live as equals. He worked toward this goal all his life. His dreams still give people hope today.

Learn about the fight for freedom. Tour the National Civil Rights Museum.

Dr. King was shot and killed on April 4, 1968.

Want to learn about famous scientist Albert Einstein? Visit the American Museum of Science and Energy.

The American Museum of Science and Energy

Meet some real robots. See how wind and water power work. Try some tests with light, sound, and electricity. Learn about science jobs you might have someday.

You're exploring the American Museum of Science and Energy! It's in Oak Ridge. So is Oak Ridge National Laboratory (ORNL). The U.S. government established this site in 1943. Scientists there helped develop **atomic** bombs. Those bombs were used in World War II (1939–1945).

Scientists at ORNL are still at work. Some are finding ways to make the air cleaner. And others are finding better sources of energy. Would you like to work at ORNL someday?

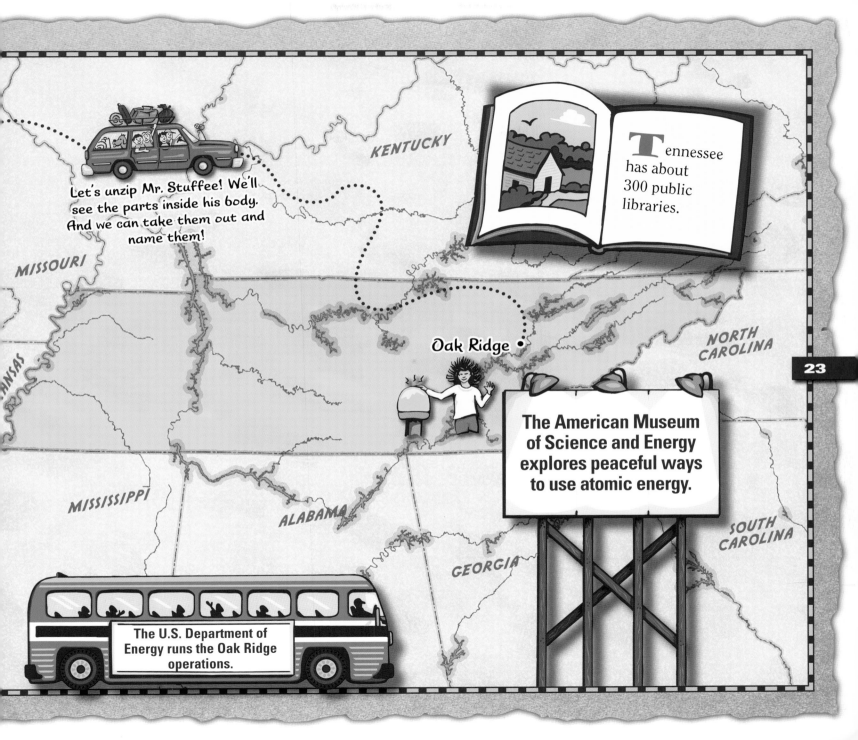

Let's unzip Mr. Stuffee! We'll see the parts inside his body. And we can take them out and name them!

Tennessee has about 300 public libraries.

Oak Ridge •

The American Museum of Science and Energy explores peaceful ways to use atomic energy.

The U.S. Department of Energy runs the Oak Ridge operations.

KENTUCKY

MISSOURI

ARKANSAS

MISSISSIPPI

ALABAMA

GEORGIA

NORTH CAROLINA

SOUTH CAROLINA

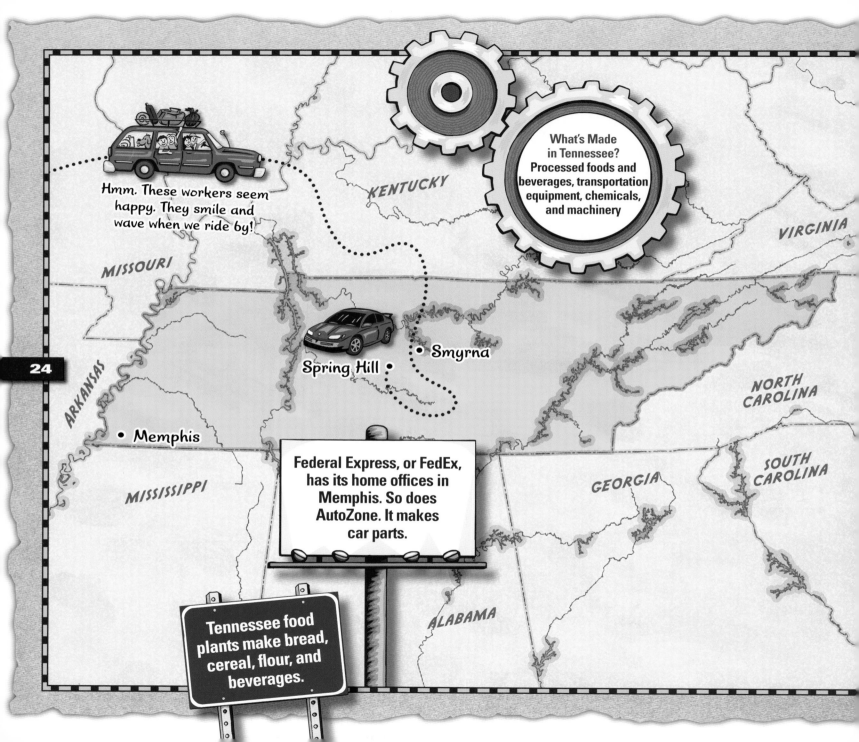

Hmm. These workers seem happy. They smile and wave when we ride by!

What's Made in Tennessee? Processed foods and beverages, transportation equipment, chemicals, and machinery

KENTUCKY

VIRGINIA

MISSOURI

ARKANSAS

Spring Hill • Smyrna

• Memphis

NORTH CAROLINA

MISSISSIPPI

Federal Express, or FedEx, has its home offices in Memphis. So does AutoZone. It makes car parts.

GEORGIA

SOUTH CAROLINA

ALABAMA

Tennessee food plants make bread, cereal, flour, and beverages.

Spring Hill's Saturn Plant

You can tour the Nissan plant in Smyrna. It makes 500,000 cars a year.

Want to see how cars are made? Just stop by Spring Hill's Saturn plant. First, you'll put on some safety goggles. Next, you'll hop on a little cart. Then off you go around the noisy factory. Car parts are moving everywhere—even overhead!

Food products are Tennessee's leading factory goods. But vehicles come in second. Tennessee factories make cars, car parts, and boats. Chemical products are important, too. They include paint, medicines, and soap.

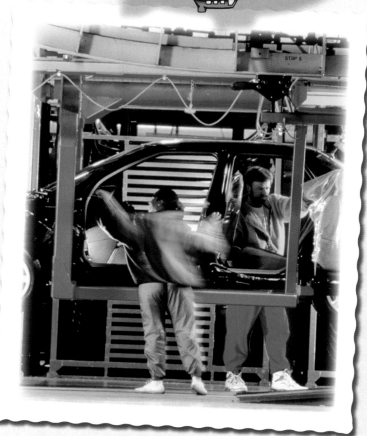

Curious about how cars are made? Head to Spring Hill's Saturn plant!

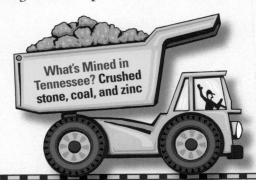

What's Mined in Tennessee? Crushed stone, coal, and zinc

General Motors is the parent company of Saturn.

The State Capitol in Nashville

It's hard to miss the state capitol. It sits high on Capitol Hill. And a tall white tower rises on top. This grand building houses important state government offices.

Tennessee's government has three branches. One branch consists of the General Assembly. Its members make the state's laws. The governor heads another branch. This branch makes sure that people obey the law. Judges make up the third branch of government. They apply the law to court cases. Then they decide whether laws have been broken.

Want to watch lawmakers in action? Just stop by the capitol in Nashville!

During the Civil War, Union troops occupied Nashville (1862–1865). They used the capitol as Fort Andrew Johnson.

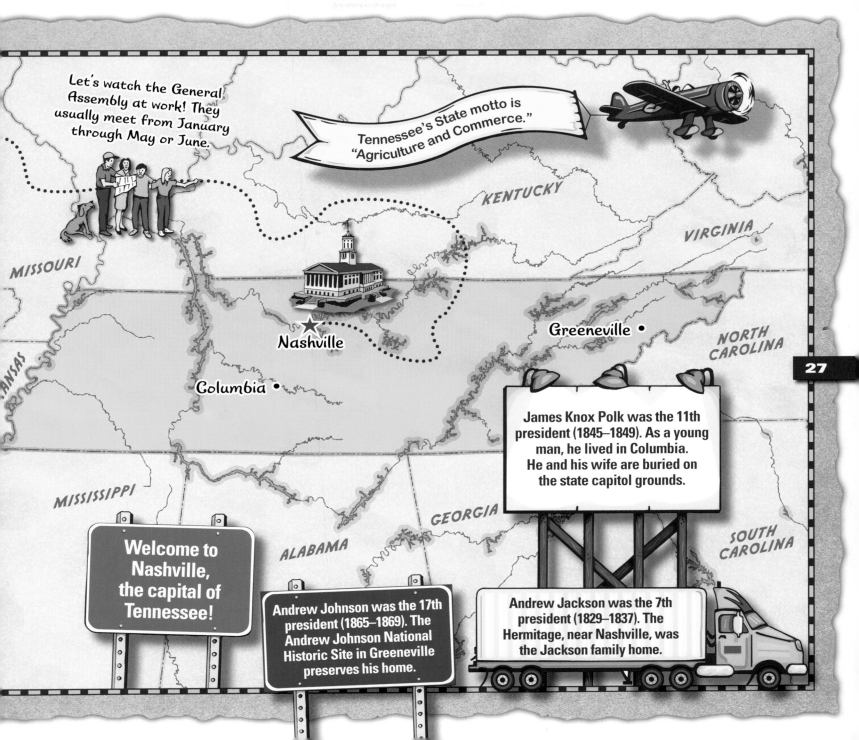

Let's watch the General Assembly at work! They usually meet from January through May or June.

Tennessee's State motto is "Agriculture and Commerce."

KENTUCKY

VIRGINIA

MISSOURI

NORTH CAROLINA

Greeneville •

★
Nashville

Columbia •

James Knox Polk was the 11th president (1845–1849). As a young man, he lived in Columbia. He and his wife are buried on the state capitol grounds.

MISSISSIPPI

GEORGIA

SOUTH CAROLINA

ALABAMA

Welcome to Nashville, the capital of Tennessee!

Andrew Johnson was the 17th president (1865–1869). The Andrew Johnson National Historic Site in Greeneville preserves his home.

Andrew Jackson was the 7th president (1829–1837). The Hermitage, near Nashville, was the Jackson family home.

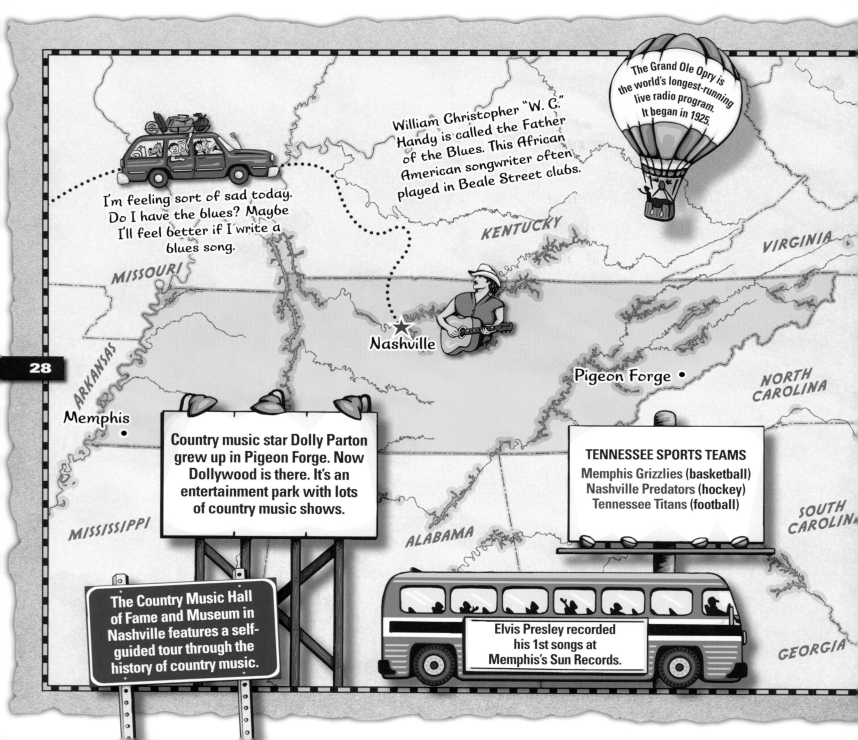

I'm feeling sort of sad today. Do I have the blues? Maybe I'll feel better if I write a blues song.

William Christopher "W. C." Handy is called the Father of the Blues. This African American songwriter often played in Beale Street clubs.

The Grand Ole Opry is the world's longest-running live radio program. It began in 1925.

Nashville

Pigeon Forge •

Memphis •

Country music star Dolly Parton grew up in Pigeon Forge. Now Dollywood is there. It's an entertainment park with lots of country music shows.

TENNESSEE SPORTS TEAMS
Memphis Grizzlies (basketball)
Nashville Predators (hockey)
Tennessee Titans (football)

The Country Music Hall of Fame and Museum in Nashville features a self-guided tour through the history of country music.

Elvis Presley recorded his 1st songs at Memphis's Sun Records.

MISSOURI

KENTUCKY

VIRGINIA

ARKANSAS

NORTH CAROLINA

MISSISSIPPI

ALABAMA

SOUTH CAROLINA

GEORGIA

On the Music Trail

Check out a concert at the Grand Ole Opry!

Many music styles found a home in Tennessee. Nashville is known for country music. The Grand Ole Opry House is there. Its country music concerts are broadcast on radio. This is where many country music stars got their start.

About 700,000 people visit Graceland every year. It was Elvis Presley's home in Memphis. Who was Elvis? The King of Rock and Roll!

Beale Street is another Memphis music spot. It's called the Home of the Blues. African American blues musicians started playing there. By the 1920s, their music became popular. Stroll down Beale Street today. You'll still hear the blues!

The Liberty Bowl takes place in Memphis around New Year's Day. It's a football game for top college teams.

Wander through the Museum of Appalachia.
Would you like to live in a mountain village?

Check out the main museum building at the Museum of Appalachia. You'll see a fiddle made from a mule's jawbone!

The Museum of Appalachia in Norris

Fiddlers and banjo pluckers play lively tunes. Vats of sweet molasses bubble away. People are churning butter and splitting logs. It's the Fall Homecoming at the Museum of Appalachia!

Appalachia is the Appalachian Mountain Region. It includes the highlands of eastern Tennessee. Many pioneers settled here in the 1700s. They had come from England, Scotland, and Ireland. They brought their music and crafts with them. They developed an Appalachian **culture** all their own.

The Museum of Appalachia is a mountain village. There you'll learn about daily life in Appalachia. Wander from one log house to another. It's fun to imagine living there!

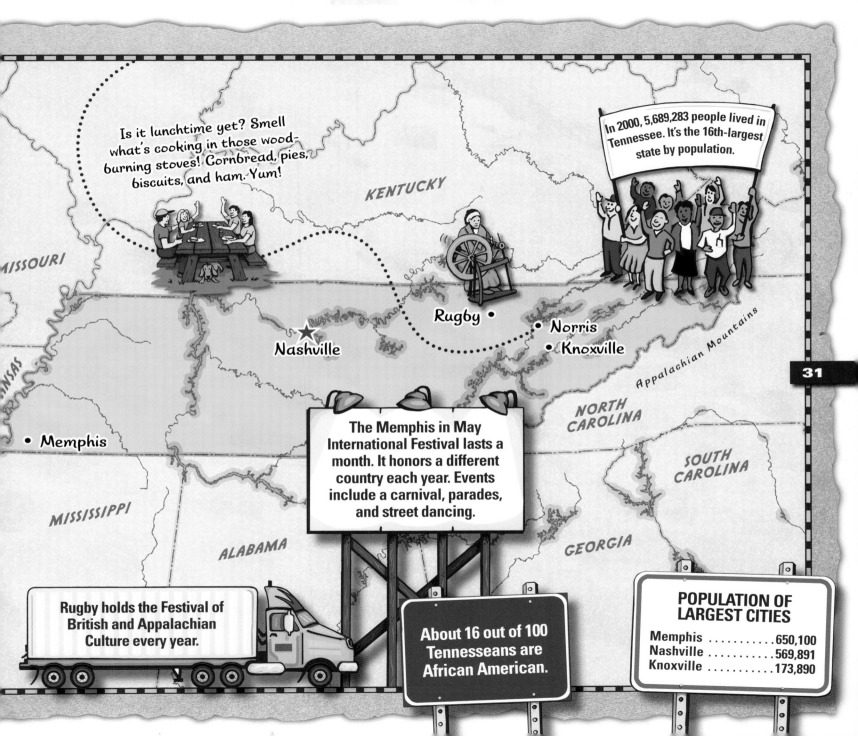

Is it lunchtime yet? Smell what's cooking in those wood-burning stoves! Cornbread, pies, biscuits, and ham. Yum!

In 2000, 5,689,283 people lived in Tennessee. It's the 16th-largest state by population.

MISSOURI

KENTUCKY

Rugby •

• Norris
• Knoxville

Nashville

Appalachian Mountains

NORTH CAROLINA

• Memphis

SOUTH CAROLINA

MISSISSIPPI

The Memphis in May International Festival lasts a month. It honors a different country each year. Events include a carnival, parades, and street dancing.

GEORGIA

ALABAMA

Rugby holds the Festival of British and Appalachian Culture every year.

About 16 out of 100 Tennesseans are African American.

POPULATION OF LARGEST CITIES

Memphis 650,100
Nashville 569,891
Knoxville 173,890

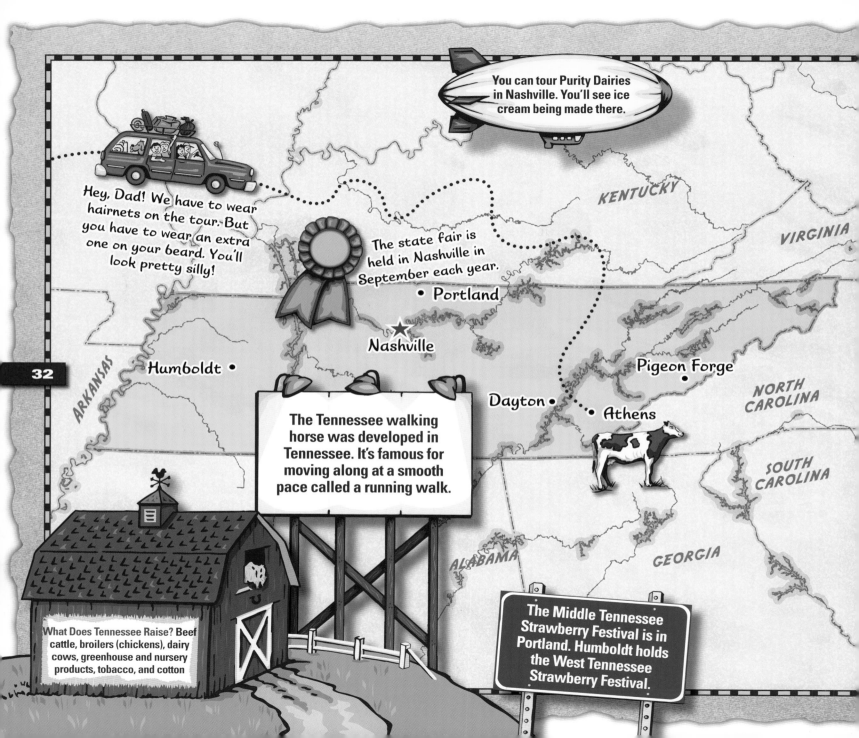

You can tour Purity Dairies in Nashville. You'll see ice cream being made there.

Hey, Dad! We have to wear hairnets on the tour. But you have to wear an extra one on your beard. You'll look pretty silly!

The state fair is held in Nashville in September each year.

The Tennessee walking horse was developed in Tennessee. It's famous for moving along at a smooth pace called a running walk.

What Does Tennessee Raise? Beef cattle, broilers (chickens), dairy cows, greenhouse and nursery products, tobacco, and cotton

The Middle Tennessee Strawberry Festival is in Portland. Humboldt holds the West Tennessee Strawberry Festival.

KENTUCKY
VIRGINIA
ARKANSAS
NORTH CAROLINA
SOUTH CAROLINA
ALABAMA
GEORGIA

Portland
Nashville
Humboldt
Pigeon Forge
Dayton
Athens

Touring Mayfield Dairy in Athens

Where does ice cream come from? You'll get the scoop at Mayfield Dairy! You'll watch trucks bringing fresh milk from farms. Then you'll watch machines heating the milk. Some milk goes into milk jugs. And some goes on to become ice cream. You'll see the process and then eat some!

Milk cows are important farm animals in Tennessee. Beef cattle and chickens are valuable, too. Many farmers raise horses or hogs.

Soybeans are the state's top crop. Farmers also grow cotton, corn, and tobacco.

Moo! Don't forget to take a tour of Mayfield Dairy!

The Old Mill at Pigeon Forge was built in 1830. It's still grinding grain with every turn of its waterwheel.

The Tennessee Strawberry Festival is in Dayton.

Moon Pie Madness!

Say hello to RC Cola and Ms. Moon Pie! These performers are part of the festival.

Have you ever had a Moon Pie? It's a yummy snack. It's made of two big chocolate-covered graham-cracker cookies. In between is a gooey marshmallow filling!

Does that sound delicious? Then come to Bell Buckle in June. You'll enjoy the RC and Moon Pie Festival. It celebrates Royal Crown (RC) Cola and Moon Pies!

Try out the Moon Pie Madness Games. Then get ready for the World's Largest Moon Pie. It's carved up in pieces. Hungry people line up to get some. So get in line early. You might come back for seconds!

Bell Buckle's population in 2000 was 391. But more than 20,000 people show up for the RC and Moon Pie Festival!

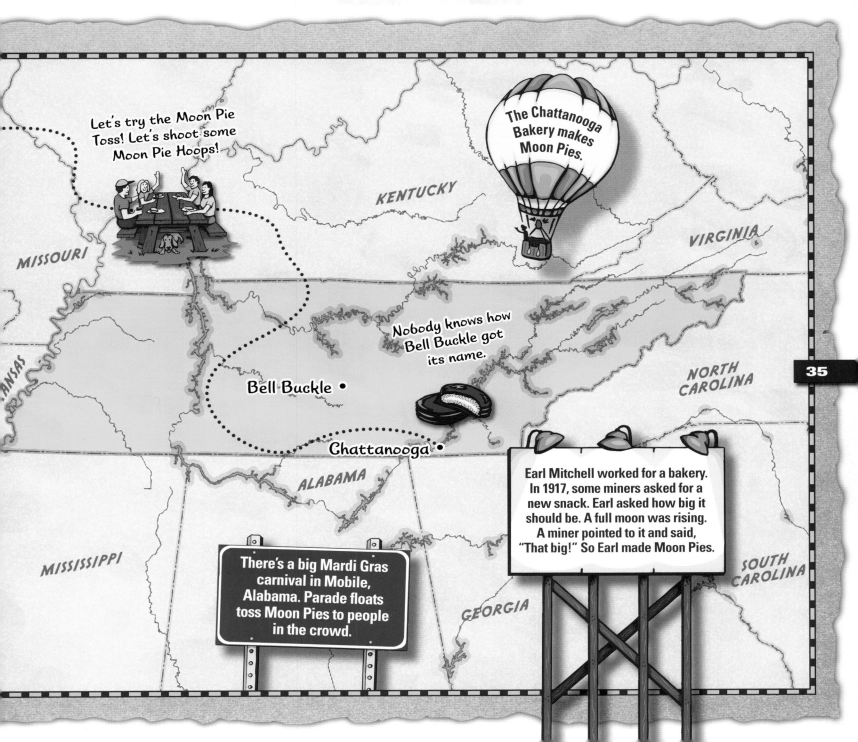

Let's try the Moon Pie Toss! Let's shoot some Moon Pie Hoops!

The Chattanooga Bakery makes Moon Pies.

KENTUCKY

VIRGINIA

MISSOURI

Nobody knows how Bell Buckle got its name.

Bell Buckle •

NORTH CAROLINA

ARKANSAS

Chattanooga •

ALABAMA

Earl Mitchell worked for a bakery. In 1917, some miners asked for a new snack. Earl asked how big it should be. A full moon was rising. A miner pointed to it and said, "That big!" So Earl made Moon Pies.

MISSISSIPPI

There's a big Mardi Gras carnival in Mobile, Alabama. Parade floats toss Moon Pies to people in the crowd.

GEORGIA

SOUTH CAROLINA

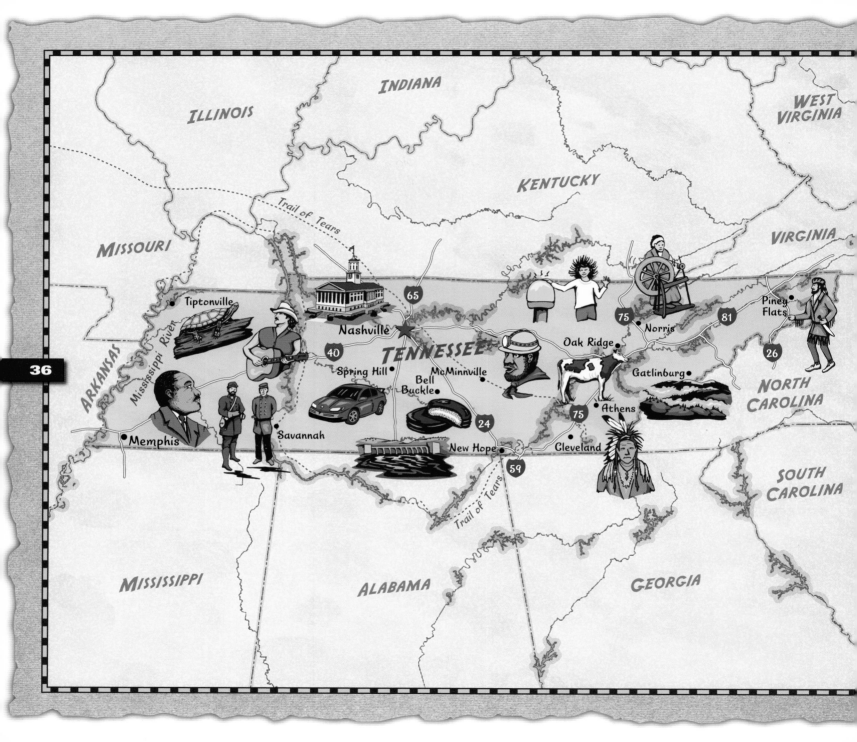

ILLINOIS

INDIANA

WEST VIRGINIA

MISSOURI

KENTUCKY

VIRGINIA

Trail of Tears

ARKANSAS

Tiptonville

Mississippi River

Nashville

65

TENNESSEE

40

Spring Hill

McMinnville

Bell Buckle

Oak Ridge

Norris

75

81

Piney Flats

26

NORTH CAROLINA

Gatlinburg

Memphis

Savannah

24

New Hope

75

Athens

Cleveland

SOUTH CAROLINA

59

Trail of Tears

MISSISSIPPI

ALABAMA

GEORGIA

OUR TRIP

We visited many amazing places on our trip! We also met a lot of interesting people along the way. Look at the map on the left. Use your finger to trace all the places we have been.

Which 3 states meet in Cumberland Gap National Historical Park? See page 6 for the answer.

What is Tennessee's official state amphibian? Page 9 has the answer.

How do wild hogs cool off? See page 11 for the answer.

Where was Davy Crockett born? Look on page 14 for the answer.

Which state had more Civil War battles than Tennessee? Page 16 has the answer.

When was Dr. Martin Luther King shot? Turn to page 21 for the answer.

What is the longest-running live radio program? Look on page 28 for the answer.

Where is the Country Music Hall of Fame? Turn to page 28 for the answer.

That was a great trip! We have traveled all over Tennessee!

There are a few places we didn't have time for, though. Next time, we plan to visit Fort Nashborough in Nashville. It was built to protect and shelter early settlers. Visitors can take historic tours and watch reenactments.

More Places to Visit in Tennessee

WORDS TO KNOW

anniversary (an-uh-VER-suh-ree) a date that marks when an important event occurred in the past

atomic (uh-TOM-ik) using power released when tiny particles called atoms are split

caverns (KAV-urnz) caves

civil rights (SIV-uhl RITES) the rights that belong to every citizen

culture (KUHL-chur) the customs, beliefs, and way of life of a group of people

erosion (ih-ROW-zhun) wearing away by water or wind

pioneers (py-uh-NEERZ) the 1st people to settle in a territory

reservoir (REZ-ur-vwar) a holding area used to store water

robots (ROW-bohts) machines that do human tasks

Tennessee covers 41,217 square miles (106,752 sq km). It's the 34th-largest state in size.

STATE SYMBOLS

State agricultural insect: Honeybee

State amphibian: Tennessee cave salamander

State bird: Mockingbird

State butterfly: Zebra swallowtail

State flower: Iris

State folk dance: Square dance

State fruit: Tomato

State game bird: Bobwhite quail

State gem: Tennessee river pearl

State horse: Tennessee walking horse

State insects: Firefly and ladybug

State reptile: Eastern box turtle

State rocks: Limestone and agate

State sport fish: Largemouth bass

State tree: Tulip poplar

State wild animal: Raccoon

State wildflower: Passion flower

38

State flag

State seal

STATE SONGS

"My Homeland, Tennessee"

Words by Nell Grayson Taylor, music by Roy Lamont Smith

Tennessee has 7 official state songs. "My Homeland, Tennessee," adopted as a state s
in 1925, is the oldest. The others are "When It's Iris Time in Tennessee," "My Tenness
"Tennessee Waltz," "Rocky Top," "Tennessee," and "The Pride of Tennessee."

O Tennessee, that gave us birth,
To thee our hearts bow down.
For thee our love and loyalty
Shall weave a fadeless crown.
Thy purple hills our cradle was;
Thy fields our mother breast
Beneath thy sunny bended skies,
Our childhood days were blessed.

'Twas long ago our fathers came,
A free and noble band,
Across the mountain's frowning heights
To seek a promised land.
And here before their raptured eyes;
In beauteous majesty:
Outspread the smiling valleys
Of the winding Tennessee.

Could we forget our heritag
Of heroes strong and brave
Could we do aught but cherish
Unsullied to the grave?
Ah no! The State where Jackson s
Shall ever peerless be.
We glory in thy majesty;
Our homeland, Tennessee.

Chorus:
O Tennessee: Fair Tennessee
Our love for thee can never di
Dear homeland, Tennessee.

FAMOUS PEOPLE

Acuff, Roy (1903–1992), country music singer

Agee, James (1909–1955), author

Crockett, Davy (1786–1836), frontiersman

Dean, Mark (1957–), inventor

Farragut, David Glasgow (1801–1870), 1st U.S. admiral

Freeman, Morgan (1937–), actor

Giovanni, Nikki (1943–), poet

Gore, Albert, Jr. (1948–), politician

Handy, W. C. (1873–1958), blues musician and composer

Jackson, Andrew (1767–1845), 7th U.S. president

Johnson, Andrew (1808–1875), 17th U.S. president

McKissack, Patricia (1944–), children's book author

Parton, Dolly (1946–), country music singer and songwriter

Pinkwater, Daniel (1941–), children's book author

Polk, James (1795–1849), 11th U.S. president

Presley, Elvis (1935–1977), rock and roll musician

Rudolph, Wilma (1940–1994), track star and Olympic medalist

Sequoyah (ca. 1775–1843), American Indian scholar

Smith, Bessie (1894–1937), blues singer

Timberlake, Justin (1981–), singer

Turner, Tina (1939–), singer

TO FIND OUT MORE

At the Library

Alphin, Elaine Marie, and Tim Parlin (illustrator). *Davy Crockett*. Minneapolis: Lerner Publications Company, 2003.

Gaines, Ann. *Andrew Jackson: Our Seventh President*. Chanhassen, Minn.: The Child's World, 2002.

Krull, Kathleen, and David Diaz (illustrator). *Wilma Unlimited: How Wilma Rudolph Became the World's Fastest Woman*. San Diego: Harcourt Brace, 1996.

McGinty, Alice B. *Meet Daniel Pinkwater*. New York: PowerKids Press, 2003.

Rumford, James. *Sequoyah: The Cherokee Man Who Gave His People Writing*. Boston: Houghton Mifflin Co., 2004.

On the Web

Visit our home page for lots of links about Tennessee:
http://www.childsworld.com/links

Note to Parents, Teachers, and Librarians: We routinely verify our Web links to make sure they are safe, active sites—so encourage your readers to check them out!

Places to Visit or Contact

Tennessee Civil War National Heritage Area
1421 East Main Street
Murfreesboro, TN 37132
615/494-8916
For more information about the history of Tennessee

Tennessee Department of Tourist Development
William Snodgrass/Tennessee Tower
312 8th Avenue North, 25th Floor
Nashville, TN 37243
615/741-9001
For more information about traveling in Tennessee

INDEX

40

Bye, Volunteer State.
We had a great time.
We'll come back soon!